Touchscreen

A Poem
by Marshall Davis Jones

Introducing the new Apple iPerson
Complete with multi-touch and volume control

Doesn't it feel good to touch?
Doesn't it feel good to touch?
Doesn't it feel good to *touch*?

Compatible with your iPod and your iPad
Doesn't it feel good to touch?
Doesn't it feel good to touch?

Your life is an app
Your strife is an app
Your wife is an app
Doesn't it feel good to touch?

My world has become so digital
I have forgotten what that feels like

It used to be hard to connect when friends formed cliques,
Now it's even more difficult to connect now that clicks form friends

But who am I to judge?
I face Facebook more than books face me
Hoping to book face-to-faces

I update my status
420 spaces
To prove I’m still breathing

Failure to do this daily means my whole web wide world would forget that I exist

But with 3,000 friends online
And only five I can count in real life
Why wouldn't I spend more time in a world where there are more people that
'like' me?

Wouldn't you?

Here, it doesn't matter if I'm an amateur person
As long as I have a 'pro' file

My smile is 50% genuine
And 50% genuine HD

You would need blu-rays to see the white on my teeth

But I'm not that focused

Ten tabs open
Hopin' my problems can be resolved with a 1600 by 1700
resolution

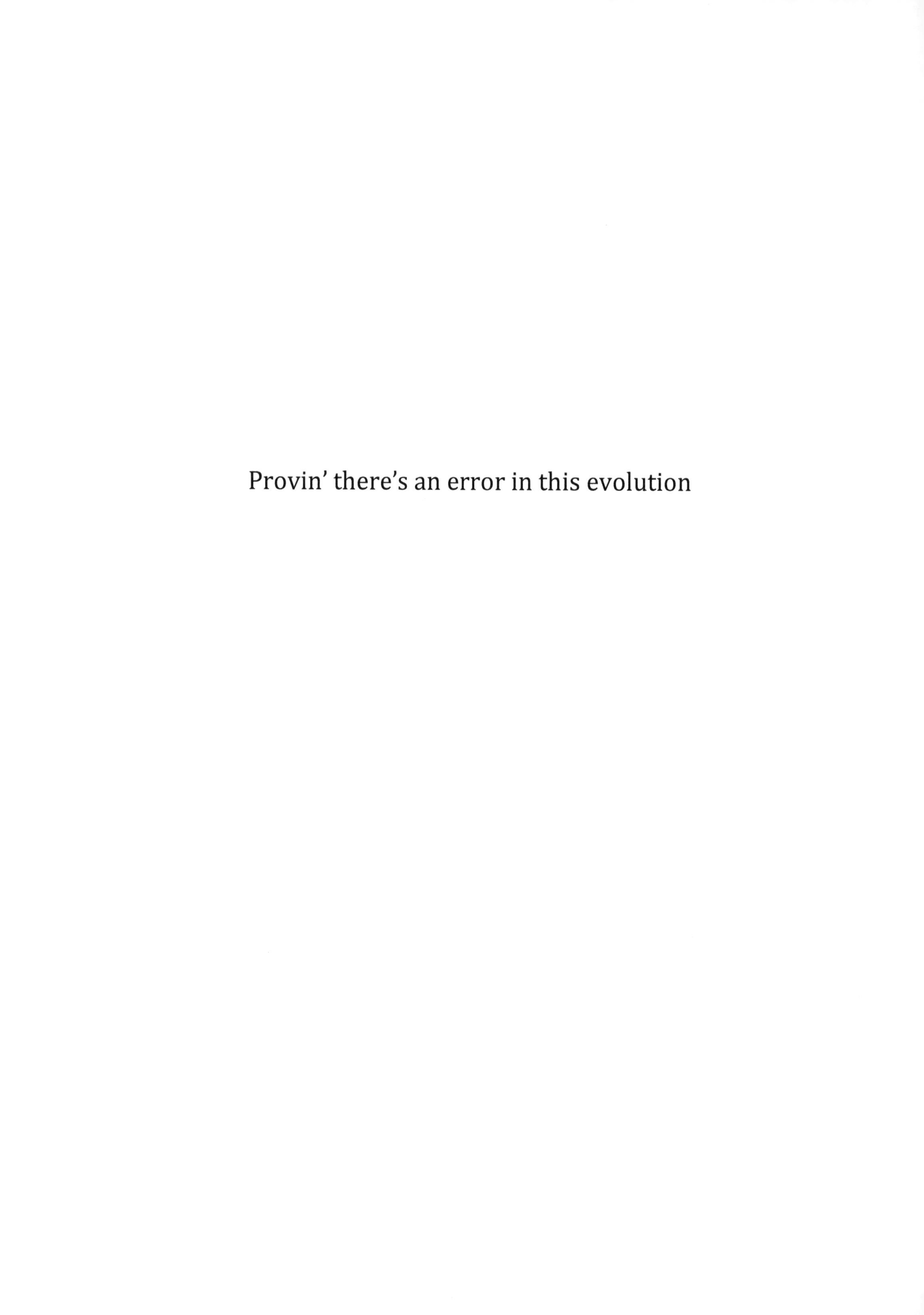
Provin' there's an error in this evolution

Doubled over we used to sit in tree tops
Till we swung down and stood upright

Then someone slipped a disc

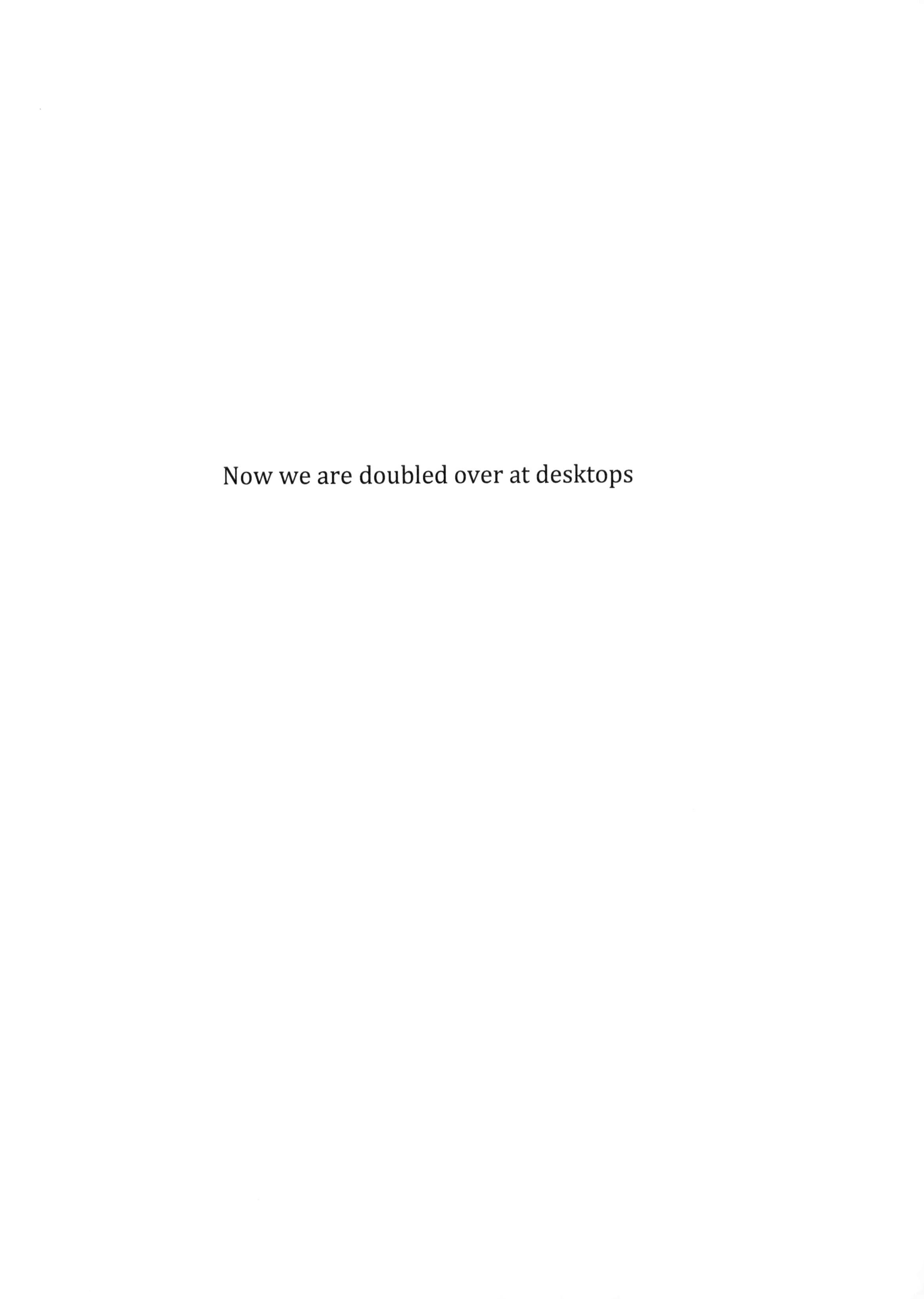

Now we are doubled over at desktops

From the Garden of Eden
To the branches of Macintosh
Apple-picking has always come at a great cost

iPod
iMac
iPhone
iChat
I can do all of these things without making eye-contact

We used to sprint to pick and store blackberries
Now we run to the Sprint Store to pick Blackberries

It's scary

Can't hear the sound of Mother Nature speaking
Over all this tweeting
And our ability to feel along with it is fleeting

You would think these headphone jacks inject in the flesh
The way we connect to disconnect

Power on
Till we are powerless

They've got us love-drugged
Like e-pills
So we E*TRADE
Email
E-motion
Like E-commerce

Because now money can buy love
For $9.95 a month
Click

To proceed to checkout
Click

To x-out where our hearts once were
Click

I've uploaded this hug, I hope she gets it
Click

I'm making love to my wife, I hope she's logged in
Click

I'm holding my daughter over a Skype conference call
While she's crying in the crib in the next room
Click

So when my phone goes off in my hip iTouch, iTouch, iTouch,
and iTouch

Because in a world where laughter is never heard
And voices are only read

We're so desperate to feel
That we hope our technologic can reverse the universe
Until the screens touch us back

And maybe one day they will

When our technology is advanced enough
To make us human again

www.ingramcontent.com/pod-product-compliance
Ingram Content Group UK Ltd.
Pitfield, Milton Keynes, MK11 3LW, UK
UKHW051134260726
13967UKWH00010B/3033

9 781312 089372